REVELATION REVOLUTION
CREATION IS WAITING

STEVE PIXLER

CONTINUUM MINISTRY RESOURCES | MANSFIELD, TX

REVELATION REVOLUTION | CREATION IS WAITING

STEVE PIXLER

Copyright (c) 2020 | Steve Pixler
All rights reserved.
Published by Continuum Ministry Resources, Mansfield, TX.
More resources available at stevepixler.com.

Unless otherwise noted, all scripture passage are quoted from:

The Holy Bible, English Standard Version® (ESV®) Copyright © 2001 by Crossway, a publishing ministry of Good News Publishers.
All rights reserved.

Scripture quotations marked TPT are from The Passion Translation®. Copyright © 2017, 2018, 2020 by Passion & Fire Ministries, Inc. Used by permission. All rights reserved. ThePassionTranslation.com.

ISBN: 978-0-9914552-3-2

INTRODUCTION

Changed people change the world.

This is the radical idea Paul taught in one of the most astonishing passages in Scripture: Romans 8. He actually said—if you can believe it!—that the entire universe will be transformed in a brilliant denouement of glory when the cosmos beholds the glory of God revealed in *us*.

I am not exaggerating this one smidgen. Paul taught with unabashed bravado that believers will be "*glorified*" when we behold the unfiltered glory of God revealed in the face of Jesus, and creation will be glorified when it beholds the glory of God in us. Quite literally, the act of beholding the infinite glory of God transforms whoever and whatever beholds it.

If a person beholding the full glory of God was not indwelled by the Spirit of God, then the glory of God would vaporize him or her in a puff. (And "after this, the judgment.") As God said to Moses, "No person can see my face—my fullest glory—and live!"

But if the person is indwelled by the Spirit of God, beholding the infinite glory of God transfigures him or her. The glory of God without unites with the glory within and explodes outward, externalizing as the image of God manifest in glorious individuality.

The only way I know how to even remotely conceptualize this is to think of how the internal pressure and structural strength of a submarine keeps the ocean from collapsing the vessel. The Presence of God within the believer creates an internal pressurization that stabilizes the heart to sustain the "eternal weight of glory." The Spirit within absorbs and conducts the energy of the matter-shattering glory of God, and the human body is supernaturally transformed into an image-bearing, glory-sharing person. They are *glorified*.

Talk about the ultimate nuclear fission event.

People are changed when they see God. That's incredible enough all by itself. But Paul's larger point about creation is nothing short of breathtaking: creation will be changed when it sees *us*. Specifically, when it sees the glory of God revealed in us. The world changes by beholding the glory of God revealed in glory-changed people—in you and me. The revolution of creation comes from the revelation of God's people. It's a *revelation revolution*.

Does anyone besides me think that's a fantastic, supernatural, science-fiction-on-steroids, crazy, cool idea?

Regardless, that's the idea I want to chew on like my seven-year-old self with some Big League Bubble Gum. Rip the package, hand me a piece, and let's get to chewing.

1

A BRISK WALK THROUGH ROMANS 8

Romans 8 is one of the most astonishing passages in the Bible. It's scope is literally cosmic. In just a few short verses, Paul describes how a vast universe writhes and groans in the birth pangs of new creation, and how the final transformation of creation will come when awestruck galaxies behold the dazzling glory of God radiating from transfigured believers.

Paul talks a lot about the glory of God, but never in more epic terms than Romans 8. The theme of glory rises throughout Romans like a symphony building to its crescendo. Romans 8 is the grand finale.

The glory of God is simply the attributes of God manifest. The glory of God is when God displays his beauty, goodness, power, wisdom, holiness, on and on. The glory of God is the essence of God unveiled. And when believers are glorified, God's likeness will shine forth from them like the sun. When creation is glorified, the entire universe will display the likeness of God, revealing his wisdom, power and goodness.

Literally, Paul teaches that the unveiling of God's glory in you and me will precipitate the cosmic regeneration of the entire creation. That really is epic.

Take a minute and read the passage from Romans 8. Now, I know it's tempting to skim the scripture passages since they are often so familiar to us. But don't skip this one. In fact, I quoted here from The Passion Translation, the freshest, most vivid translation out these days, just so you could read Romans 8 with new eyes. It's worth it!

Here's the key passage:

> I am convinced that any suffering we endure is less than nothing compared to the magnitude of glory that is about to be unveiled within us. The entire universe is standing on tiptoe, yearning to see the unveiling of God's glorious sons and daughters!
>
> For against its will the universe itself has had to endure the empty futility resulting from the consequences of human sin. But now, with eager expectation, all creation longs for freedom from its slavery to decay and to experience with us the wonderful freedom coming to God's children. To this day we are aware of the universal agony and groaning of creation, as if it were in the contractions of labor for childbirth.
>
> And it's not just creation. We who have already experienced the firstfruits of the Spirit also

inwardly groan as we passionately long to experience our full status as God's sons and daughters—including our physical bodies being transformed. For this is the hope of our salvation.

But hope means that we must trust and wait for what is still unseen. For why would we need to hope for something we already have? So because our hope is set on what is yet to be seen, we patiently keep on waiting for its fulfillment. (Romans 8:18–24 TPT)

Isn't that incredible?! All that talk about the glory that shall be unveiled in us and creation standing on tiptoe like an excited child at a parade straining to see the children of God coming into view—that's a beautiful, vivid picture.

All of this will happen at the resurrection when Jesus comes again. Yet, as we shall see, everything that will happen in the resurrection when Jesus comes again has already begun in the world through the resurrection of Jesus in the middle of history. The revolution has already begun!

So, here's what we need to do for a moment: let's look at what shall happen then in order to better understand what is happening now. By clarifying our expectations for then, we can sharpen our expectations for now.

That will make more sense in a moment.

The Second Coming

Here and elsewhere, Paul and other New Testament writers lay out a three step revelation that shall occur when Jesus returns.

(1) Jesus shall *appear* and his blinding glory shall be revealed.

(2) Believers will *behold* his glory and be instantly transformed, revealing the glory of the Lord.

(3) Creation will *behold* the glory of God manifest in believers and be universally glorified.

The revelation of God's glory in the face of Jesus will transform believers, and the revelation of God's glory in the face of believers will transform creation.

John the apostle described this *revelation revolution*:

> Beloved, we are God's children now, and what we will be has not yet appeared; but we know that when he appears we shall be like him, because we shall see him as he is. (1 John 3:2)

We are already God's children, but it is not yet apparent what our body shall be like in the resurrection when we are glorified. But we know when Jesus is revealed we will be like him—get this!—"because we shall see him as he is."

Seeing Jesus as he is is the catalyst of glorification. We are transformed by and in the act of beholding him.

I remember wondering when I was a kid how Jesus would glorify so many people all at once when he comes again. Would it be the "cry of command," the "voice of an archangel," maybe "the sound of the trumpet of God"? (1 Thessalonians 4:16) Maybe the trumpet would hit a certain timbre that would shatter corruption like brittle yellow glass?

Then, while reading 1 John 3:2, I saw what was actually there: "We shall be like him, because we shall see him as he is."

The process of transformation actually occurs when the fullness of glory is revealed in the face of Jesus. As God told Moses, "No one can see my face and live." To see the glory of God in its fullness is to be consumed by his power and majesty. Like the "lawless one" whom "the Lord Jesus will kill with the breath of his mouth and bring to nothing by the appearance of his coming" (2 Thessalonians 2:8).

But we who are hidden in Christ will not be consumed by the glory of God; rather, the glory of God will glorify us.

As Paul said,

> Listen, and I will tell you a divine mystery: not all of us will die, but we will all be transformed. 52 It will happen in an instant —in the twinkling

of his eye. For when the last trumpet is sounded, the dead will come back to life. We will be indestructible and we will be transformed. 53 For we will discard our mortal "clothes" and slip into a body that is imperishable. What is mortal now will be exchanged for immortality. (1 Corinthians 15:51–53 TPT)

It is breathtaking to consider how powerful the glory of God really is. In just one glimpse of his glory—literally, just "the wink of an eye"!—whoever beholds the Father's glory is forever changed.

But that one glimpse of glory is just the first glance. The second glance—again, in the "wink of an eye"—will be the brilliant flash of glory when transformed and raptured saints erupt into earth's atmosphere like the blinding light of a billion rising suns, and creation beholds "the unveiling of God's glorious sons and daughters." In one moment, the glory of God will bolt like lightning from one end of the universe to the other, and every atom of the cosmos will explode with infinite light. The entire universe will be instantly, eternally, magnificently transformed. All creation will be born again.

We will be changed when we see him glorified. Creation will be changed when it sees us glorified.

That's how change occurs.

What's Coming Has Come

And that's how Paul believed that change would occur forever when Jesus comes again. Yet not for one moment did Paul believe that this change was postponed until the Second Coming. Paul believed the change that was coming had already come.

Though Paul was a strong advocate for "the blessed hope," for the expectation of the Second Coming and the resurrection; and though Paul argued fiercely against the "fulfilled eschatologies" of his day, the doctrines that taught "that the resurrection is past already"; yet Paul steadfastly believed that the future had already broken in upon human history with the resurrection of Jesus. Paul believed that the kingdom of God was already inaugurated in the resurrection, ascension and effusion of the Spirit at Pentecost. The future was already here.

Paul and his compadres believed that the kingdom of God was what modern scholars like to call "already/not yet," that the kingdom came into the middle of history with the incarnation of Jesus and introduced the future into history to guarantee our destiny.

In other words, the future resurrection was pulled back into the middle of history when Jesus rose from the dead, and what shall be in the age to come has already begun in the present. This is why Jesus came to earth in the middle of history!

When we received the Holy Spirit, we received what Hebrews calls "the power of the age to come." The Holy Spirit is the "earnest of our inheritance," the "down payment" on eternity. This means that heaven, which shall come to earth in fullness when Jesus comes again, has already started breaking in upon the world now.

Jesus said, "If I by the finger of God do cast out devils, then the kingdom of God has come upon you." Jesus also said that his kingdom is not "of this world," which means that it comes from heaven into earth. Jesus also said "the kingdom of God is within you." And Paul added that "the kingdom of God is not meat and drink, but righteousness, peace and joy in the Holy Spirit."

All of this shows that the kingdom to come has already started coming in the world with the incarnation, resurrection and ascension of Christ and the outpouring of the Holy Spirit at Pentecost.

Why does this matter? Why does it matter that Paul believed that the kingdom has already started manifesting in the world prior to the Second Coming?

Simply this. Paul believed that the transformation of creation had already begun. Paul believed that the revelation revolution had already begun.

For example, Paul believed both that death had been defeated at the cross and that it would be defeated finally at the Second Coming. Look at this:

[Our] Savior Christ Jesus, who abolished death and brought life and immortality to light through the gospel. (2 Timothy 1:10)

Then comes the end, when he delivers the kingdom to God the Father after destroying every rule and every authority and power. For he must reign until he has put all his enemies under his feet. The last enemy to be destroyed is death. (1 Corinthians 15:24–26)

Jesus "abolished death." Yet death is the "last enemy to be destroyed."

Which is it? Both.

Both are true. Jesus abolished death, but death remains an enemy for us that shall be finally and fully defeated when Jesus returns.

This is just one of many indications that Paul and the early church believed that they lived in the overlap of ages, that they saw themselves as living a reality that had already broken in upon the world but would not fully complete until the resurrection when Jesus comes again.

Yet—gosh darn it!—they would have *never* believed the pablum that so many Christians have bought into these days that we are meant to just hunker down in the corner and hold on until things finally can't get any worse and Jesus comes back to rescue his poor beleaguered, bedraggled bride.

Poppycock.

In Greek.

And Hebrew.

And English, for that matter.

Paul believed that the world would be transformed in finality when Jesus comes again. He believed that the transfiguration of creation would be a global—nay, universal event!—that would fulfill every promise God ever made about the restoration of creation. No doubt.

But Paul also believed that the world was being transformed now. He knew that Jesus commissioned his disciples to preach the gospel—the good news of salvation—to "all creation." Paul knew that our message of good news was to all the cosmos. As he said in Colossians 1:23, we preach "the hope of the gospel that you heard, which has been proclaimed in all creation under heaven."

In all *creation*. Not just the people on the planet, but the planet itself. "The earth is the Lord's and the fullness thereof; the world and those who dwell therein" (Psalm 24:1). Never has the gospel been about saving a few people from the earth, and then abandoning God's good creation once a full load of souls have been gathered up.

Paul believed that we should preach to all creation the good news that it would share in the glorious freedom of the children of God. As Jesus commissioned the disciples, "Go into all the world and proclaim the gospel to the *whole creation*" (Mark 16:15). This is the full, universal scope of the gospel of the kingdom.

And Paul believed that the coming glory was already breaking in upon the world. As Paul also said in Colossians 1:27, Jesus is "Christ in you the hope of glory." Because the hope of glory is already in you, there is hope of glory all around you. You are meant to be salt and light.

The point is simply this: the reality spoken of in Romans 8—that the world is transformed when it beholds the glory of God in us—is a reality that is already present and perfecting within the world. We are not meant to wait until the Second Coming to expect the kingdom of God to change the world.

That's *why* Jesus went away into heaven—to multiply his Presence in us and accomplish through us what could not be accomplished without us. As Jesus said, "It is expedient for you that I go away." He also said that we would do greater works than him *because* he was going to the Father.

This means that the process of world-transformation has already begun in us. Jesus is not waiting until he comes again to advance his rule in the world over the nations. He is doing so through us now. When he does come again, it will be because the work of saving the lost, building his ekklesia and destroying the works of the devil is finished.

As Paul said in 1 Corinthians 15, Jesus will subdue all his enemies under his feet before he returns and defeats death, the "last enemy." The return of Jesus is the Grand Finale, the Final Act, the crescendo of kingdom victory.

So, grasp these two ideas with both hands:

(1) The world will be changed forever when it beholds the glory of God revealed in us.

(2) The world is changed *now* as we reveal the glory of the Lord—world-change is not postponed until the Second Coming.

The revelation revolution has already begun.

So let's take a moment and look closer at *revelation*.

2

REVELATION

Creation is transformed when it beholds the glory of the Lord in you and me. That's the Big Idea. We reveal the glory after we behold the glory and are transformed into the likeness of God. The revelation of God *to* us becomes the revelation of God *through* us. So, world transformation flows out of revelation. It's a revelation revolution.

First, we should define revelation. My little pop-up iPad dictionary is helpful here: revelation is "the making known of something that was previously secret or unknown." Works for me. God bless Apple.

Revelation is "*apokalupsis*" in the Greek, and it literally means "to unveil," to pull back a curtain. When Paul prays that the Ephesians would receive a "spirit of wisdom and revelation," he is asking Holy Spirit to yank the cord on the curtain and reveal what God is doing in the world. Curtains up!

Just like creation will be transformed ultimately when believers are glorified eternally, so the world around us is changed now when the curtain of our life is pulled back just enough to reveal the goodness of God. As Jesus said, "That they may see your good works and glorify your Father, which is in heaven." Just a glimpse of God's goodness in our world brings powerful change.

Revelation is revolutionary.

2 Corinthians 3 & 4

Now, if revelation is revolutionary, then we need to think a bit about revelation. How does it work? Let's start with this: the process of revelation is three-fold.

(1) We *behold* the glory of the Lord.

(2) We are *transformed* into the likeness of God.

(3) We *manifest* the glory we now carry.

Paul lays it out in brilliant detail:

> But when one turns to the Lord, the veil is removed. Now the Lord is the Spirit, and where the Spirit of the Lord is, there is freedom. And we all, with unveiled face, beholding the glory of the Lord, are being transformed into the same image from one degree of glory to another. For this comes from the Lord who is the Spirit. (2 Corinthians 3:16–18)

Here's the first two steps in verse 18: (1) *beholding* and (2) *transforming*. The third step, *manifesting*, is a few verses down as Paul continues:

> And even if our gospel is veiled, it is veiled to those who are perishing. In their case the god of this world has blinded the minds of the unbelievers, to keep them from seeing the light of

the gospel of the glory of Christ, who is the image of God. For what we proclaim is not ourselves, but Jesus Christ as Lord, with ourselves as your servants for Jesus' sake. For God, who said, "Let light shine out of darkness," has shone in our hearts to give the light of the knowledge of the glory of God in the face of Jesus Christ. (2 Corinthians 4:3–6)

And there's the third step in verse 6: we manifest glory as we "give the light of the knowledge of the glory of God in the face of Jesus Christ."

So think back through how Paul explained the process of revelation:

We behold the glory of God with an unveiled face. In other words, the veil of deception is removed by the Holy Spirit, the Spirit of freedom, and we clearly see Jesus revealed in the Law and Prophets. In that moment of revelation, Jesus fully manifests the truth about the Father that the Law had obscured and distorted through fleshly misperception.

As John said,

> For from his fullness we have all received, grace upon grace. For the law was given through Moses; grace and truth came through Jesus Christ. No one has ever seen God; the only God, who is at the Father's side, he has made him known. (John 1:16–18)

Jesus reveals the Father. And we are transformed as we see the truth about him. For most Christians today, our blindness—the lies we have believed about God—comes from Christian tradition, the formalism of dead religion, more than the Law of Moses. But religion is religion wherever it is. And when Jesus breaks those lies with truth, we are set free to know Father God for who he really is. "You shall know the truth and the truth shall make you free."

We behold the glory of God when we behold the truth about God. In fact, there is a direct connection between beholding the glory of God and seeing the truth about his goodness. When Moses asked to see the glory of God, God declared that he would cause his goodness to pass before him. When the lies we have believed about God—specifically, slanders against his goodness—are exposed, then the truth about the Father revealed in Jesus sets us free. We are transformed.

This is why inner healing always flows out of exposing lies we have believed about God and embracing the truth about him. Every sin we commit is rooted in a lie we believe.

That started with Adam and Eve in the Garden: they believed the serpent's lie about God, about them and about the fruit. Ever since that fateful day, every sin, every bad habit, every addiction, every act of evil —all of it!—flow out of lies we've believed. This is why deep spiritual, soulish and physical healing always come out of replacing lies with truth. Always.

When we break off the lies and embrace the truth, change manifests. People around us can see the difference that the glory of God makes in us as we are transformed. We become a living, walking, talking revelation.

The love of God manifest in our life pulls back the curtain on delusions about God and exposes the lies others have believed about him. The glory of God shines out of us "to give the light of the knowledge of the glory of God in the face of Jesus Christ." When people around us behold the glory of the Lord through us, their perception of God changes. To put it simply—this is how changed people change the world.

Matthew 16

The connection between revelation and revolution is drawn explicitly in Matthew 16. In this passage, Jesus takes his disciples into "the district of Caesarea Philippi," and asks them the surprising question, "Who do people say I am?"

The disciples looked quizzically at each other and stammered, "Uh, people say different things. Some say you're John the Baptist, some say Elijah or one of the prophets." They paused expectantly, wondering where this was going.

Now, just before Jesus answers, we need to take a quick look at our surroundings. It is no accident that Jesus brought his disciples to this infamous Roman city. Built in honor of the Emperor, Caesarea Philippi was the crown jewel of ancient Palestine, and its streets swirled with the confluence of the three dominant cultures that shaped the Mediterranean world of Jesus' day: the Jewish, Greek and Roman cultures.

Where Jesus stood speaking to his disciples lay in the shadow of Mt. Hermon, the fabled mountain of Jewish mythology where the fallen angels conspired to corrupt the earth. Just to Jesus' left was the yawning mouth of the Grotto of Pan, the world-famous shrine to the dark god of the underworld. This cavern was called "The Gates of Hell."

Not a nice place.

We need to take the measure of our environs in Matthew 16 because Jesus' choice of location says so much about the implications of revelation and revolution. Jesus could have taken his disciples to a Bible camp somewhere in the wilderness. He could have drawn them off into a quiet corner of the temple in Jerusalem. He could have taken them on a peaceful cruise across the lake. There were countless options for repose and reflection.

But Jesus stood them dead center of the most hostile religious, political and cultural environment he could possibly have chosen. Caesarea Philippi was definitely the enemy's camp. And it's right here, smack dab in the middle of the devil's playground, that Jesus issues the ultimate kingdom challenge: "Upon this rock I will build my church and the gates of hell shall not prevail against it." Bold, strident words.

But we're getting ahead of ourselves. We need to glance back at Jesus' questions: "Who do people say I am? And who do you say I am?" These questions are profoundly significant. Jesus wanted to know that the disciples had fully grappled with what the world thought about him and what they had come to believe about him. Wish-washy opinions borrowed from others can never fuel a revolution. Only deep conviction can.

The revolution will come in the real world. And you can't get any more real world than Caesarea Philippi. But the only thing that will revolutionize the real world is a revelation.

"Who do you say I am?" Jesus asked. Simon Peter rose to answer the question: "You are the Christ, the Son of the living God."

Good answer. Right answer. But it was actually much more than just a good answer, a right answer. It was a revelation. As Jesus put it,

> "Blessed are you, Simon Bar-Jonah! For flesh and blood has not revealed this to you, but my Father who is in heaven."

Simon didn't put it all together, simply add two-plus-two and come up with four, on his own. His confession of faith was an outburst of divine insight. Father God opened his eyes and revealed it to him. Simon was catching his first wide-eyed look at the glory of God revealed in the face of Jesus Christ. And, as he beheld, awestruck Simon was being transformed:

> And I tell you, you are Peter, and on this rock I will build my church, and the gates of hell shall not prevail against it. I will give you the keys of the kingdom of heaven, and whatever you bind on earth shall be bound in heaven, and whatever you loose on earth shall be loosed in heaven."

Jesus changed Simon's name to "Peter," which meant "a stone." Simon, the son of Jonah—named after the cowardly prophet who fled from the Lord—was becoming a rock on which Jesus could build his church. And this transformation started with a revelation. Simon started becoming Peter when he saw the glory of God in the face of Jesus: "You are the Son of God!"

Then notice what happened to the revelation. It became a two-edged sword. The same revelation that unveiled the glory of God in the face of Jesus started unveiling the image of God in the face of Peter. Peter needed transformation.

Peter was called to be Jesus' "key man" in the kingdom, but he just wasn't ready for that yet. And he didn't become fully ready until after he had walked through rebuking the Lord; fussing with his brothers over who would the greatest; protesting futilely that he would never deny the Lord; trying in vain to defend Jesus with the sword; denying after all that he knew him; weeping bitterly in remorse; abandoning his call and returning back to fishing; comparing himself bitterly to John; and only God knows what else.

Peter was called, but he wasn't ready. He needed the other side of revelation—the side that unveiled his heart and transformed him in light of God's glory. Peter needed not only to "know God," but to "be known of God." Peter needed Pentecost.

So do we.

This part of the revelation is supremely difficult, but transformation starts here when God "the Searcher of hearts" starts revealing the true self we were meant to be.

> Do not lie to one another, seeing that you have put off the old self with its practices 10 and have put on the new self, which is being renewed in knowledge after the image of its creator. (Colossians 3:9-10)

Revelation is all about identity. It's all about God's identity revealed to us, and our identity revealed to the world. And this exchange of identity occurs when we are drawn into relationship with God.

And the revelation relationship that unveils identity also forms community. "Upon this rock I will build my church." The community of faith is built on the rock of revelation, the rock of identity. In this mutual exchange of knowing, God brings his covenant people together into revelation relationship with one another. "We shall know even as we are known."

As I experience revelation relationship—knowing and being known of God—he brings me into revelation relationship with you, for you are also knowing and being known of God. I meet you in him. Literally, you are hidden in Christ and so am I. "Fancy meeting you here!" I find me and you in Christ.

In fact, I cannot truly know Christ without agreeing to know you. I cannot love God without loving you. Sink down slowly and soak in this powerful word:

> Beloved, let us love one another, for love is from God, and whoever loves has been born of God and knows God. Anyone who does not love does not know God, because God is love. (1 John 4:7–8)
>
> We love because he first loved us. If anyone says, "I love God," and hates his brother, he is a liar; for he who does not love his brother whom he has seen cannot love God whom he has not seen. And this commandment we have from him: whoever

loves God must also love his brother. (1 John 4:19–21)

This is such an important word, especially for prophetic types who seek revelation relationship with God but withdraw from revelation relationship with others due to rejection.

People can be painful. I get it. Believe me. But we must grasp the central role that the revelation of community plays in the revelation of the glory of God to the world.

Individual "revelators" here and there cannot "fill the earth with the knowledge of the glory of the Lord as the waters cover the sea." Only a "multitude no one can number" can do that. Kingdom revolution requires a revelation community. It's all about the power of two or three, the exponential power of divine/human agreement.

"By this all people will know that you are my disciples, if you have love for one another." (John 13:35)

The revelation revolution happens when the world sees a unified church. Jesus' deepest prayer was that "they all may be one." And this is why Satan fights to divide the church more than anything else he does. It is his top priority. Why? Because a divided church fragments the revelation of the glory of God, and the manifestation of the glory is the catalyst for world transformation. Creation is liberated from the curse when the glorious sons and daughters of God are unveiled. Satan works to stop this at all costs.

Our identity grows as we discover our true self in God and others. Revelation relationship draws out aspects of God's being in the unique manifestation of God in others. I see God in you. Then, I am fleshed out in my identity through my interaction with you. I embody the revelation. You bring out dimensions of me that I never saw before. I see more of me in you. Then, I see more of you in God and me. This circular revelation of identity grows in interchange of community.

But there's more. As my identity grows in community through the revelation of God, self and others, I enter new dimensions of authority related to my gifts and calling. Identity in community releases authority.

Authority in the kingdom flows out of who I am in Christ and how I am related to others in the kingdom. This is why the New Testament speaks so much about loving one another, serving one another and submitting to one another. It's also why Jesus modeled authority by washing the disciples' feet.

Look at Luke's account of how Jesus taught them:

> A dispute also arose among them, as to which of them was to be regarded as the greatest. And he said to them, "The kings of the Gentiles exercise lordship over them, and those in authority over

them are called benefactors. But not so with you. Rather, let the greatest among you become as the youngest, and the leader as one who serves. For who is the greater, one who reclines at table or one who serves? Is it not the one who reclines at table? But I am among you as the one who serves. (Luke 22:24-34)

Who will be the greatest? The one who serves. The one who serves whom? Others. Authority is gained by developing identity as we serve in community. Kingdom authority flows upside down. (Actually, right side up—the world is upside down.) It's inverse promotion: humble yourself to be exalted.

In fact, authority in the kingdom is conferred. Authority comes from "the laying on of hands." This means that authority comes from our relationship with others in the kingdom.

Even Paul, the most independent of all apostolic mavericks, was sent from Antioch on his missionary journeys by the kingdom community. He also went back to Jerusalem to confirm his teaching and mandate with the "pillars" of the church. (Galatians 1, 2) Paul believed in submission to authority in order to receive authority.

Sadly, this idea has been grievously abused. Yet the principle remains: authority grows in community.

Jesus went on,

"You are those who have stayed with me in my trials, and I assign to you, as my Father assigned to me, a kingdom, that you may eat and drink at my table in my kingdom and sit on thrones judging the twelve tribes of Israel.

Jesus was passionate about his disciples discovering identity in community that develops into authority because the advance of his kingdom depends on it. The revolution requires revelation, and revelation requires relationship.

The apostles were "assigned a kingdom," and they would "sit on thrones judging the twelve tribes of Israel." But before they could sit on thrones, they had to sit at the table. They had to learn how to get along as brothers, as a family. The table of communion always precedes the throne of dominion.

Jesus understood perfectly how corrupting total power really is. In fact, Jesus refused to build his kingdom on power—he was determined to build it on love. The only way to keep the kingdom of God from being corrupted by power was to make sure that all authority in the kingdom flows from love for one another, submission to one another and service for one another.

We've all suffered church hurts that happened when leaders exercised authority from power instead of love, when they tried to rule without submission to other believers. Authority over without authority under is tyranny.

Then, Jesus wrapped up his Luke 22 discourse on authority by addressing Simon Peter, the same Simon that had such a powerful revelation in Caesarea Philippi:

"Simon, Simon, behold, Satan demanded to have you, that he might sift you like wheat, but I have prayed for you that your faith may not fail. And when you have turned again, strengthen your brothers."

This was the moment of truth for Simon. He had beheld the glory of God in the face of Jesus Christ; but now the light of God's truth was about to expose hidden parts of Simon he really didn't want anyone to know—in fact, things that he didn't even believe were true about him. Simon was about to be known.

But in the heart of this warning lies a great promise: "When you have turned again..." Jesus already knew the outcome! Peter's faith would not fail because his faith was the faith of Jesus himself, the faith given as a gift by the heavenly Father. Peter would be alright because he had a revelation. Or, better yet, the revelation had him.

Herein lies the revolutionary power of the revelation: the revelation carries within itself the power to create revolution. Whatever water touches gets wet—water carries wetness as an inherent quality. The same is true of revelation: whoever sees God's glory is changed. Transformation is the inherent quality of revelation. If you didn't change, you didn't see him. The revelation of Jesus is a self-fulfilling prophecy.

We must strengthen our brothers. We must embody the revelation as we are transformed by the glory of God. As we are transformed by the glory, our capacity to carry the glory is increased. Our capacity for serving others is increased. Our capacity for kingdom responsibility is increased. We are strengthened through testing and we strengthen others through our testimony. We "turn again" and help others make it through.

As Father God sees that we are tested and trusted to serve others in love, he releases us into realms of greater authority in the kingdom. This is favor. He opens new metrons of kingdom responsibility. We can be trusted with his power because we have been tested by his love.

Remember Jesus' question for Simon after he went back to fishing? "Peter, do you love me more than these?" All Jesus wanted to know was if Peter loved him. Nothing else mattered. The revelation revolution is rooted in love—love for God, love for people.

This is how we receive the keys of the kingdom. We grow into the purpose for which we were saved, and we are given keys that unlock the gates of hell, open the strongholds, bind the strongman and deliver the captives. As we are transformed, we step into the kingdom authority we have been given.

When we exercise that authority, we release the shalom of God into our metron ("area of influence") and "the knowledge of the glory of the Lord fills the earth as the waters covers the sea." When we are transformed, the nations are transformed. That's a revolution!

Changed people change the world.

3

REVOLUTION

Let's talk about the revolution. What will the world look like when the kingdom comes?

First of all—as I said before—there's no doubt that the fullness of the kingdom awaits the Second Coming. Paul is clear that there is a change coming to you and me at the end of history that will precipitate cosmic, universal transformation:

> I tell you this, brothers: flesh and blood cannot inherit the kingdom of God, nor does the perishable inherit the imperishable.
>
> Behold! I tell you a mystery. We shall not all sleep, but we shall all be changed, in a moment, in the twinkling of an eye, at the last trumpet. For the trumpet will sound, and the dead will be raised imperishable, and we shall be changed. For this perishable body must put on the imperishable, and this mortal body must put on immortality. When the perishable puts on the imperishable, and the mortal puts on immortality, then shall come to pass the saying that is written: "Death is swallowed up in victory." (1 Corinthians 15:50–54)

The resurrection of believers will be the catalyst for the resurrection of all creation.

Firstfruits and Fullness

Hold that idea with one hand. Then, with the other hand, grasp the other idea that Paul also argues over and over: the kingdom has already broken into the world through the resurrection of Jesus two-thousand years ago. The kingdom is coming, but the kingdom is already here.

Paul sets up this contrast between the "already" and the "not yet" in the language of "firstfruits" and "fullness":

> And not only the creation, but we ourselves, who have the firstfruits of the Spirit, groan inwardly as we wait eagerly for adoption as sons, the redemption of our bodies. (Romans 8:23)

> He who descended is the one who also ascended far above all the heavens, that he might fill all things...until we all attain to the unity of the faith and of the knowledge of the Son of God, to mature manhood, to the measure of the stature of the fullness of Christ. (Ephesians 4:10, 13)

The outpouring of the Holy Spirit is the firstfruits of the coming kingdom; the future resurrection and new creation is the fullness of the kingdom. This means that what is coming should already be coming here and now. The revolution that shall happen in fullness when Jesus comes again is the revolution that is happening now in a firstfruits sense.

Think about firstfruits and fullness for a second: the firstfruits of a harvest is quantitatively different from the full harvest but qualitatively the same. In other words, the firstfruits of an apple harvest is still apples. Fewer apples, yes, but still apples.

The firstfruits of an apple harvest wouldn't be crabapples. Which is silly, but is also exactly the same sort of silliness proposed by an eschatology that expects the kingdom to win after Jesus comes but lose until then. Or an eschatology that "spiritualizes" the kingdom now and postpones its physical expression until after the Second Coming.

No, whatever the kingdom will be when Jesus returns is what it has already started becoming now. No doubt there will be a fullness of victory when Jesus comes, but we should expect the firstfruits of victory now. There will be a fullness of physical manifestation in the earth when Jesus comes, but we should expect the firstfruits of kingdom manifestation now.

The Second Coming is the grand finale, the crescendo, of victory. Christ's First Advent was the inauguration of his everlasting kingdom and his Second Advent will be its consummation.

All this language—firstfruits/fullness, already/not yet, inauguration/consummation—are intended to show us that the surprising resurrection of Jesus in the middle of history has brought the future back into the middle and released it as the catalyst of world transformation here and now.

There's more.

Adoption

Paul uses the metaphor of a child growing into maturity to exemplify how the kingdom comes in the world. He describes the first coming of Christ, his resurrection, ascension and effusion of the Spirit—the First Advent—as the birth pangs of the new age. He then describes the resurrection of all things, the glorification of our bodies, the liberation of creation—the Second Advent—as an "adoption."

> And not only the creation, but we ourselves, who have the firstfruits of the Spirit, groan inwardly as we wait eagerly for adoption as sons, the redemption of our bodies. (Romans 8:23)

Two ideas, birth and adoption. We who are "born again" long for "adoption." What the heck does he mean by that? If we are born again, then why do we need to be adopted? If God is our Father, then why does he need to adopt us?

The answer is simple. The word "adoption" here is actually "*huiothesian*," which means "to be set in place as a son." Adoption in this context is not a father adopting a non-biological son as his child; rather, it is a father recognizing his biological son as his heir and as a citizen of the city. He is "set in place as a son."

Here's the point: adoption in Bible times happened long after birth. And the example that Paul is carrying forward in this passage is that the resurrection of Jesus and the outpouring of the Holy Spirit at Pentecost is the new birth of believers and the Second Coming will be our adoption as full grown sons and daughters.

Just another way of saying "already/not yet."

We are sons and daughters of God; yet we await the fullness of our redemption when our bodies are immortalized in the resurrection. Yet we do not wait until we are immortal to walk in our new reality, in the holiness of heaven. That's Paul's entire point in Romans 6-8: you are already saved now, so live like it. The same is true of the kingdom: what is coming has already come. So live like it.

Inauguration/consummation; firstfruits/fullness; birth/adoption. All of these are ways of describing the "already/not yet" of the kingdom. And all of this to explain how the future has already broken in upon history and that world transformation is already happening.

On Earth As It Is In Heaven

Whatever Scripture tells us to expect in the new creation should already be appearing in the world.

Whatever "heaven" will be like when it comes to earth in the new creation should be exactly the sort of heaven that we are praying into earth right now: "Let it be on earth as it is in heaven."

What is heaven like? That's what we're praying for on earth. Now.

This is humongotastically important because it radically defines our kingdom expectation between now and the Second Coming. If we postpone the victory of Christ's kingdom until after the Second Coming, then we will have zero expectation now for world transformation. We will look around at the world going to hell in a hand-basket, "Tsk, tsk," reproachfully, and pray for the rapture.

But if we believe that what is coming has already come, then we will expect heaven to transform earth now. We will expect salt and light to influence the world now. We will expect nothing short of a revolution—a revelation revolution. Which is exactly what we should expect.

What Revolution Looks Like

So what will the revolution look like?

Like this:

> It shall come to pass in the latter days that the mountain of the house of the Lord shall be established as the highest of the mountains, and shall be lifted up above the hills; and all the

nations shall flow to it, and many peoples shall come, and say: "Come, let us go up to the mountain of the Lord, to the house of the God of Jacob, that he may teach us his ways and that we may walk in his paths."

For out of Zion shall go forth the law, and the word of the Lord from Jerusalem. He shall judge between the nations, and shall decide disputes for many peoples; and they shall beat their swords into plowshares, and their spears into pruning hooks; nation shall not lift up sword against nation, neither shall they learn war anymore. O house of Jacob, come, let us walk in the light of the Lord. (Isaiah 2:2–5)

And like this:

On this mountain the Lord of hosts will make for all peoples a feast of rich food, a feast of well-aged wine, of rich food full of marrow, of aged wine well refined.

And he will swallow up on this mountain the covering that is cast over all peoples, the veil that is spread over all nations. He will swallow up death forever; and the Lord God will wipe away tears from all faces, and the reproach of his people he will take away from all the earth, for the Lord has spoken. (Isaiah 25:6–8)

More (don't skim this one!):

For behold, I create new heavens and a new earth, and the former things shall not be remembered or come into mind. But be glad and rejoice forever in that which I create; for behold, I create Jerusalem to be a joy, and her people to be a gladness.

I will rejoice in Jerusalem and be glad in my people; no more shall be heard in it the sound of weeping and the cry of distress. No more shall there be in it an infant who lives but a few days, or an old man who does not fill out his days, for the young man shall die a hundred years old, and the sinner a hundred years old shall be accursed.

They shall build houses and inhabit them; they shall plant vineyards and eat their fruit. They shall not build and another inhabit; they shall not plant and another eat; for like the days of a tree shall the days of my people be, and my chosen shall long enjoy the work of their hands. They shall not labor in vain or bear children for calamity, for they shall be the offspring of the blessed of the Lord, and their descendants with them.

Before they call I will answer; while they are yet speaking I will hear. The wolf and the lamb shall graze together; the lion shall eat straw like the ox, and dust shall be the serpent's food. They shall not hurt or destroy in all my holy mountain," says the Lord. (Isaiah 65:17–25)

On and on and on. Isaiah's prophecies about the new creation are the most famous, but the Old Testament is chock full of promises like this.

Then the New Testament writers take these beautiful prophecies of the new creation and apply them to now.

For example, in 2 Corinthians 6:2, Paul quotes from Isaiah 49:8, a prophecy about the new creation:

> For he says, "In a favorable time I listened to you, and in a day of salvation I have helped you."

Then Paul says the "day of salvation" is happening now:

> Behold, now is the favorable time; behold, now is the day of salvation.

What is Paul saying? Simply that the foretold new creation has already begun to break in upon the world right now.

Peter said the same sort of thing in Acts:

> And all the prophets who have spoken, from Samuel and those who came after him, also proclaimed these days. (Acts 3:24)

The prophets "proclaimed these days," the events surrounding Christ's resurrection and Pentecost. The revolution that the prophets foretold had already begun in the world.

John saw the new creation in his famous vision on Patmos:

> Then I saw a new heaven and a new earth, for the first heaven and the first earth had passed away, and the sea was no more. And I saw the holy city, new Jerusalem, coming down out of heaven from God, prepared as a bride adorned for her husband.
>
> And I heard a loud voice from the throne saying, "Behold, the dwelling place of God is with man. He will dwell with them, and they will be his people, and God himself will be with them as their God. He will wipe away every tear from their eyes, and death shall be no more, neither shall there be mourning, nor crying, nor pain anymore, for the former things have passed away."
>
> And he who was seated on the throne said, "Behold, I am making all things new." (Revelation 21:1–5)

John saw the heavenly city that is to come. Yet both Paul and the writer of Hebrews spoke of the coming city in the present tense:

> Now Hagar is Mount Sinai in Arabia; she corresponds to the present Jerusalem, for she is in slavery with her children. But the Jerusalem above is free, and she is our mother. (Galatians 4:25–26)
>
> But you have come to Mount Zion and to the city of the living God, the heavenly Jerusalem, and

to innumerable angels in festal gathering, and to the assembly of the firstborn who are enrolled in heaven, and to God, the judge of all, and to the spirits of the righteous made perfect, and to Jesus, the mediator of a new covenant, and to the sprinkled blood that speaks a better word than the blood of Abel. (Hebrews 12:22–24)

The heavenly city that is still to come has already started coming in the world through the gospel of the kingdom.

Examples abound of new creation prophecies being applied here and now in the New Testament. This is why—once again!—New Testament scholars say that kingdom eschatology in the New Testament is an "already/not yet" eschatology.

I am belaboring the point.

But belaboring the point is exactly what's needed these days. Too many Christians have been trained to think that the revolution will come only after Jesus returns. It will indeed come in fullness after he returns. But it is here already as firstfruits.

This means—more belaboring!—that we should expect the revolution to take root in the world right now. We should expect the first crop of apples. (And stop expecting crabapples!) We should expect that life as we shall know it then will become life as we know it now in a firstfruits sense.

What should we expect?

Salvation for the lost. Forgiveness for the repentant. Healing for broken families. Recovery for the addicted. Delivery for the captives. Prosperity for the poor. Food for the hungry. Housing for the homeless. Justice for the oppressed. Equality for the sexes. Education for the unlearned. Wisdom for the foolish. Freedom for the imprisoned. Patronage for the creative. Investments for the entrepreneurial. Good stewardship for the environment. Opportunity for the hardworking. Love for the outcasts. Healing for the sick. Health for the diseased. New beginnings for losers. Liberty for the enslaved. Rescue for the trafficked. Jubilee for the indebted. Hope for the hopeless. Peace for the war-torn. Reconstruction for the devastated. Truth for the deceived. Shalom for the nations.

On and on.

In the resurrection, transformation will happen on a personal, familial and societal level. Culture will manifest the glory of the Lord. Holiness will pervade the air we breathe, the life we lead and the relationships we enjoy. Music, art, movies and all other forms of creativity will honor the Creator. The beauty of holiness will transform the global, cultural aesthetic.

Architecture will reflect the multifaceted individuality of the Creator. The genius of God will be embodied in the economy, science, space exploration, medicine, business, government, politics—and every other human, cultural pursuit. Everything will bring glory to God through glorified humanity.

Ecology, the environment, husbandry, agriculture and all other forms of dominion over creation will manifest the wisdom, power and love of God. Never again will humans abdicate their humble dominion in exchange for greedy domination. Money will be a tool, a resource, to use for the glory of God rather than an artificial glory sought to manufacture synthetic human significance.

There will be no hunger, no war. No homeless people. No exploited women. No violence, no robbery, no rape, no molestation of little children. No more lust for sexual expression outside of covenantal, creational love. No gender confusion and sexual compulsion. Every human on the planet—indeed, in the universe! —will be fully indwelled by the Presence of the one true God. As Paul said, "God will be all in all."

And more. Much more. All the more that heaven can provide. And all that shall be then is the standard for what should be now. Then is what we're reaching for now. Then is the ideal for now. Until Jesus returns, our cry remains: "Let it be on earth as it is in heaven!"

Built for Revolution

We were built for revolution. In fact, every revolution in world history—whether political, military, economic, cultural, medical, religious, or any other—

had as it goal the transformation of the world. The need to "change the world" is embedded in the human psyche. We were created for dominion, and we all know deep down that the world was not meant to be like it is. The longing to "make the world a better place" is hardwired into our soul.

The problem is, however, that humans were the source of the problem. The world is a mess because we messed it up. The curse came upon creation because of human sin:

> For against its will the universe itself has had to endure the empty futility resulting from the consequences of human sin. (Romans 8:20)

Before Christ came, humans were caught in a cosmic Catch-22: since we were the source of the problem, we alone could fix the problem. Yet, because we were the source of the problem, we could not fix the problem. We were trapped in our own dilemma.

This is why Jesus came as a human. By becoming a human, he took on our responsibility for fixing our problem. Yet, because his Father was God, he did not share in the Adamic root, the sinful nature, that sabotaged the human fix to the human problem.

And so, by dying in our place, he confronted the problem—sin and death—and by baptizing us into his new humanity, we were made free from the problem. And when we were made free from the problem, we were liberated to be problem-solvers.

By beholding the glory of God in the face of Jesus, we are changed into his image and likeness. Then, we manifest the glory of the Lord into the world around us, and the world is changed.

As Paul said (read every phrase—every word hums with revelatory resonance!):

> Christ's resurrection is your resurrection too. This is why we are to yearn for all that is above, for that's where Christ sits enthroned at the place of all power, honor, and authority! Yes, feast on all the treasures of the heavenly realm and fill your thoughts with heavenly realities, and not with the distractions of the natural realm.
>
> Your crucifixion with Christ has severed the tie to this life, and now your true life is hidden away in God in Christ. And as Christ himself is seen for who he really is, who you really are will also be revealed, for you are now one with him in his glory!
>
> Live as one who has died to every form of sexual sin and impurity. Live as one who died to diseases, and desires for forbidden things, including the desire for wealth, which is the essence of idol worship. When you live in these vices you ignite the anger of God against these acts of disobedience.
>
> That's how you once behaved, characterized by your evil deeds. But now it's time to eliminate

them from your lives once and for all—anger, fits of rage, all forms of hatred, cursing, filthy speech, and lying. Lay aside your old Adam-self with its masquerade and disguise.

For you have acquired new creation life which is continually being renewed into the likeness of the One who created you; giving you the full revelation of God. In this new creation life, your nationality makes no difference, or your ethnicity, education, or economic status—they matter nothing. For it is Christ that means everything as he lives in every one of us! Colossians 3:1–11 (TPT):

"You have acquired new creation life." The new creation is already in you. As Paul said:

Therefore, if anyone is in Christ: new creation! The old has passed away; behold, the new has come. (2 Corinthians 5:17–19)

New creation! "The new has come." Then Paul tells us what this here-and-now new creation means for the world:

All this is from God, who through Christ reconciled us to himself and gave us the ministry of reconciliation; that is, in Christ God was reconciling the world to himself, not counting their trespasses against them, and entrusting to us the message of reconciliation. (2 Corinthians 5:18-19)

We have received "new creation life." Thus we release that reality into the world around us. We have been given the "ministry" and "message" of reconciliation. We preach new creation, and we mediate new creation.

Changed people change the world.

The passages quoted above from Colossians 3 and 2 Corinthians 5 are "let it be on earth as it is in heaven" passages. Paul clearly urges us to live now in light of the world to come. We are revolutionized by the indwelling Holy Spirit, and we become revolutionaries. And as we are transformed into the "new creation life," we mediate revelation to the world. We display the glory of God to creation, and creation is transformed.

Revelation brings revolution.

4

THE GOAL IS GLORY

One final thing before we wrap up. The goal is glory. The goal of the revolution is the glory of God. As Paul said, "Christ in you is the hope of glory" (Colossians 1:27). The revolution into which we were enlisted is a worldwide revolution of the manifest glory of God.

Here is the "slogan" of the revelation revolution:

For the earth will be filled with the knowledge (revelation) of the glory of the Lord as the waters cover the sea. (Habakkuk 2:14)

The glory of the Lord—the manifest attributes of God—transforms everything it touches. This is how the world changes. And if we understand that—that the revelation of glory is how the world changes—then that's how we will work to bring change in every area of life.

Most people seek change by tinkering with life around its edges. They try to fix broken marriages by focusing on new, memorized behaviors. They try to solve the world's problems with education, economic policy, government assistance, political solutions, medical intervention, environmental preservation, on and on. All these solutions may be noble of themselves, but they cannot fix the heart of the matter—and the heart of the matter is the heart.

Until the human heart is transformed by the glory of God, people will always revert back to form. The only way to change the world across all societal boundaries and through ongoing generations is to come humbly before the throne of God in true repentance and behold the glory of the Lord. When we behold his glory, we are transformed. And when we are transformed, we manifest the glory of God that transforms the nations around us.

Want a healed marriage? Seek the glory of the Lord. Want racial reconciliation? Seek the glory of the Lord. Want economic justice? Seek the glory of the Lord. Want criminal justice reform? Environmental stewardship? Want to end pornography, alcoholism, drug addiction, human trafficking? Fill in the blanks.

If we want to change the world, we must be changed. We must come before his Presence and humble ourselves before his brilliant face. Worship him. Exalt him. Extol him. Magnify him. Give him thanks. Praise him. Bless him. And behold him. Behold his goodness. Behold his beauty. Behold his justice. Behold his wrath against sin. Behold his fierce anger against all that dehumanizes his precious children and corrupts his magnificent planet.

I am not trying to oversimplify. I have no desire to be trite and cliched. But I know that Paul's teaching here is true: the world can only be liberated from the curse by the transformative power of God's infinite glory.

We need the glory of God now more than ever.

Groaning For Glory

All creation groans for glory. Yearns for it. Cries for it. In fact, the convulsions of the earth are groans for glory. Natural disasters—earthquakes, hurricanes, cyclones, tornadoes, volcanoes, on and on—are all cosmic protests against the corruption of sin. Governments call natural disasters "Acts of God," but they are more acts of a desperate planet struggling against the chains of sin and death.

Read again what Paul said:

> The entire universe is standing on tiptoe, yearning to see the unveiling of God's glorious sons and daughters! For against its will the universe itself has had to endure the empty futility resulting from the consequences of human sin. But now, with eager expectation, all creation longs for freedom from its slavery to decay and to experience with us the wonderful freedom coming to God's children. To this day we are aware of the universal agony and groaning of creation, as if it

were in the contractions of labor for childbirth. (Romans 8:19-22)

Creation groans for glory. But, in fact, there are several layers of groaning in Romans 8.

(1) Creation groans (vs. 19-22)

(2) Believers groan (vs. 23-25)

(3) Holy Spirit groans (vs. 26-28)

Look at the verses describing how the Holy Spirit groans with us as we pray in the Spirit:

> And in a similar way, the Holy Spirit takes hold of us in our human frailty to empower us in our weakness. For example, at times we don't even know how to pray, or know the best things to ask for. But the Holy Spirit rises up within us to super-intercede on our behalf, pleading to God with emotional sighs (groans) too deep for words.
>
> God, the Searcher of the heart, knows fully our longings, yet he also understands the desires of the Spirit, because the Holy Spirit passionately pleads before God for us, his holy ones, in perfect harmony with God's plan and our destiny.
>
> So we are convinced that every detail of our lives is continually woven together to fit into God's perfect plan of bringing good into our lives, for we are his lovers who have been called to fulfill his designed purpose. (Romans 8:26-28)

Creation groans unwillingly under the crushing curse of sin and death. Believers take hold of that groaning through intercession and transform the groans of despair into groans of hope. Creation sits up, takes notice of the hope we carry and then rises eagerly—breathlessly!—on tiptoe, leaning forward to see the manifest sons and daughters of God marching in grand parade.

But we do not intercede alone. Holy Spirit takes hold of our human weakness—when we do not know how to pray as we should!—and prays for us in perfect alignment with the will of God. Just as Jesus groaned at the tomb of Lazarus, and again in Gethsemane, the Holy Spirit groans with us, for us and as us. Our prayers are lifted up into heaven through the mediation of Christ "who is at the right hand of God, who indeed is interceding for us" (Romans 8:34).

The groans of creation, mixed with the groans of redeemed humanity, intensified by the groans of the Holy Spirit, rise into the heavens and pull heaven and earth together in one. The everlasting intercession of Jesus in the heavens releases the eternal purpose of God into earth and "all things work together for good" (Romans 8:28).

Groans of despair are transformed into groans of hope. Hope shifts the atmosphere of every room, every city, every realm of human life. (As Bill Johnson says, "The person with the most hope has the most influence.") Intercessors stand astraddle heaven and earth like a cosmic colossus and pull heaven and earth into alignment, into the "purpose, which [God] set forth in Christ as a plan for the fullness of time, to unite all things in him, things in heaven and things on earth" (Ephesians 1:9–10).

Groans of despair are transformed into groans of hope when we catch a glimpse of redemption, when we see the purpose for suffering. When we see, as Paul put it, "that any suffering we endure is less than nothing compared to the magnitude of glory that is about to be unveiled within us" (Romans 8:18). Imagine being able to evaluate your suffering as "nothing" compared to the glory of God being revealed in you.

(Next time trouble comes, just cut your eyes sideways and say, "Ah, that's nuthin'." That should be fun.)

When we behold the glory of God revealed in the face of Jesus, once marred, broken and now-glorified, we see glory that only comes through suffering. And that revelation transforms us.

Here's more on suffering and glory:

> But we have this treasure in jars of clay, to show that the surpassing power belongs to God and not to us. We are afflicted in every way, but not crushed; perplexed, but not driven to despair; persecuted, but not forsaken; struck down, but not destroyed; always carrying in the body the death

of Jesus, so that the life of Jesus may also be manifested in our bodies. For we who live are always being given over to death for Jesus' sake, so that the life of Jesus also may be manifested in our mortal flesh. So death is at work in us, but life in you. (2 Corinthians 4:7–12; 16-18)

The treasure of the Holy Spirit is carried within our still-mortal bodies—"jars of clay." And this demonstrates that "the surpassing power belongs to God and not to us." And when we go through times of deep suffering, we do so that the life of Jesus may be manifest.

Paul continues,

> So we do not lose heart. Though our outer self is wasting away, our inner self is being renewed day by day. For this light momentary affliction is preparing for us an eternal weight of glory beyond all comparison, as we look not to the things that are seen but to the things that are unseen. For the things that are seen are transient, but the things that are unseen are eternal.

"We do not lose heart." We suffer. We groan. But we do not lose heart. Why? Because we have a revelation of the eternal purpose of God manifest through suffering. We understand this unbelievable, breathtaking idea:

"Our light momentary affliction is preparing for us an eternal weight of glory beyond all comparison."

What we go through right now is actually the building materials of our eternal reward. Our suffering is developing our capacity for glory. Look at the contrast Paul makes: "Our light, momentary affliction" compared to "an eternal weight of glory." Here's the chiastic structure:

Light < Weight

Momentary < Eternal

Affliction < Glory

Literally, people, Paul is saying that what we go through now produces what we shall inherit then.

This changes everything.

If we understand that our present suffering is just testing—certification!—for greater glory, then everything we go through we go through with hope because we can see through it.

And when we see that truth—when we get the revelation that we are first tested then trusted—we mediate that revelation to the world around us. We give hope because we have hope. "Such as I have, I give to you!" (Acts 3:6).

In the next section of 2 Corinthians, Paul talks again about groaning for glory, about longing to be immortalized and glorified:

> For we know that if the tent that is our earthly home is destroyed, we have a building from God, a house not made with hands, eternal in the heavens. For in this tent we groan, longing to put on our heavenly dwelling, if indeed by putting it on we may not be found naked.
>
> For while we are still in this tent, we groan, being burdened—not that we would be unclothed, but that we would be further clothed, so that what is mortal may be swallowed up by life. He who has prepared us for this very thing is God, who has given us the Spirit as a guarantee. (2 Corinthians 5:1-5)

God "has given us the Spirit as a guarantee." We already have the "power of the age to come" dwelling within us now. Yet we groan. Why? Because we live every day in the "already/not yet." The Holy Spirit draws us inexorably toward the resurrection.

This is so important. The world around us is crying for help. Creation longs to be free. Humans everywhere all over the planet know instinctively that they were created to be "crowned with glory and honor and set over the works of God's hands." Every human heart cries for meaning, for purpose, for eternal significance. Crying for a revolution.

And only those who groan redemptively with Christ through the power of the Holy Spirit can offer help to the helpless, hope to the hopeless. We have solutions. We have answers. We have hope.

And it all begins with a wordless, guttural cry that rumbles up from deep inside our spirit and pours out as Spirit-filled intercession. We take hold of the groaning of creation, the cries for help and hope that echo from every nation under heaven; we release the groans of our own aching, yearning heart; and we surrender the mingled incense of our mutual groaning to the Holy Spirit, who gathers our groaning and interprets our pain to the Father through the solidarity of Christ's intercession for us. Jesus knows what we're feeling, for "he is a high priest who can be touched with the feelings of our weaknesses."

"Jesus wept."

And the groaning of creation invites the supernatural intervention of the Creator of heaven and earth. The Lord God of Armies hears the cry of nations and sends forth his angel armies to make war in the heavens and bind the evil powers that oppress God's good creation. Believers are selected and sent into every nation to message and minister reconciliation. The kingdom of God advances into families, cities and nations. The veil of darkness that lies over the nations is pierced by the light of the gospel. Revolution happens.

Changed people change the world.

And all of this started with a long look at the glory of God revealed in the face of Jesus Christ. That long look exposed once deluded believers to the truth that forever transforms. The believer staggers out of the Presence of God a new creation. Again and again.

And that new creation walks out into the streets of an old creation announcing the good news that new creation has come. Old creation trembles with hope and cries for deliverance. Atmospheres shift, demons flee. Strongholds are broken, strongmen are bound. Culture morphs into a reflection of redeemed humanity, and the New Jerusalem comes one day closer.

All because somebody prayed, "Let it be on earth as it is in heaven."

Changed people change the world.

5

CONCLUSION

Remember the Big Idea that drives everything we've talked about: we are transformed when we behold the glory of God in the face of Jesus, and creation is transformed when it beholds the glory of God in us.

I am not "just preaching," as the old evangelist used to say, when I say this. I mean it. Creation changes when we change. Changed people change the world. And we change when we behold the glory of God. This means that you and I cannot be satisfied with anything less than the indescribable, ineffable glory of God.

The hope of the world is the glory of God.

"If our gospel is hid, it is hid to them that are lost, for the god of this world has blinded their minds..." But sometimes I wonder if the god of this world hides the glorious gospel behind a shallow, fleshly church that presents religious performance without eternal glory. It would be awful to think that we are the veil hiding the light of God's glory. There would be nothing more criminal than for those assigned to reveal God to conceal him. Wow, that's sobering, isn't it?

Paul warned about those who embrace a "form of godliness but deny the power thereof." That's not you and me, is it? "Form-without-power" is the textbook definition of religion. Are we guilty of dead religion?

You know, even "Spirit-filled," charismatic congregations can devolve into religion. I was reared up in a hardcore, Oneness Pentecostal group, and I can tell you, loud and fast doesn't necessarily mean glorious. We learned all sorts of religious forms that looked powerful just because they were emotionally charged and performed with high intensity. Emotional can still be formal.

The question is—are we being changed? If we didn't change, we didn't see his glory. His glory always changes us. And this is why we must insist on nothing less than a full encounter with the Presence of God. Nothing less than the revelation of his glory. Nothing less than a revelation revolution.

The world is crying for help, crying for hope. We must answer. I am writing this in July, 2020 during the COVID-19 crisis. It's been a long time since we felt such global convulsions. Probably not since World War II. Maybe 1968 comes close.

COVID-19 was just the crest of a wave—a tsunami! —that has been building for long time. The "Me, too" movement; Harvey Weinstein; Jeffrey Epstein; economic upheaval; racial unrest; the Trump-contra-mundo political campaign—there seems to be no normal limits to the crazy. It's truly been an unprecedented year.

And in the middle of it all is a world groaning for glory. Right now, more than ever, we need a restoration of the glory of God. Judgment always begins at the house of God, and we need righteous judgment in God's house. We need discernment to see what God is doing. We need a revival of the glory of God in Western churches. It's time to abandon the humanistic attempts to build the church in our cleverness and church growth savvy. We need a genuine move of God.

Creation is groaning for glory. Are you? Do you feel a deep hunger inside for heaven to break through into earth? Are you exhausted with flesh-driven, human-powered churches? Then let's gather our strength in the Holy Spirit and release an intercessory groan for glory that will rattle the foundations of heaven. Let's cry out together for an invasion of earth by heaven.

Let's ask for a revelation revolution.

Made in the USA
Columbia, SC
25 September 2022